EARTH'S ENERGY EXPERIMENTS

BIOFUEL ENERGY
PROJECTS

Easy Energy Activities for
Future Engineers!

JESSIE ALKIRE
CONSULTING EDITOR, DIANE CRAIG, M.A./READING SPECIALIST

Super Sandcastle

An Imprint of Abdo Publishing
abdopublishing.com

abdopublishing.com

Published by Abdo Publishing, a division of ABDO, PO Box 398166, Minneapolis, Minnesota 55439. Copyright © 2019 by Abdo Consulting Group, Inc. International copyrights reserved in all countries. No part of this book may be reproduced in any form without written permission from the publisher. Super SandCastle™ is a trademark and logo of Abdo Publishing.

Printed in the United States of America, North Mankato, Minnesota
052018
092018

THIS BOOK CONTAINS RECYCLED MATERIALS

Design and Production: Mighty Media, Inc.
Editor: Liz Salzmann
Cover Photographs: Mighty Media, Inc.; Shutterstock
Interior Photographs: iStockphoto; Mighty Media, Inc.; Shutterstock; Wikimedia Commons

The following manufacturers/names appearing in this book are trademarks: Ball®, Karo®, Planters®, Pyrex®, Red Star® Quick-Rise™, Scotch®, Sharpie®, Stanley®, SuperMom's®

Library of Congress Control Number: 2017961698

Publisher's Cataloging-in-Publication Data

Names: Alkire, Jessie, author.
Title: Biofuel energy projects: Easy energy activities for future engineers! / by Jessie Alkire.
Other titles: Easy energy activities for future engineers!
Description: Minneapolis, Minnesota : Abdo Publishing, 2019. | Series: Earth's energy experiments
Identifiers: ISBN 9781532115608 (lib.bdg.) | ISBN 9781532156328 (ebook)
Subjects: LCSH: Biomass energy--Juvenile literature. | Handicraft--Juvenile literature. | Science projects--Juvenile literature. | Biotechnology--Experiments--Juvenile literature.
Classification: DDC 333.9539--dc23

Super SandCastle™ books are created by a team of professional educators, reading specialists, and content developers around five essential components—phonemic awareness, phonics, vocabulary, text comprehension, and fluency—to assist young readers as they develop reading skills and strategies and increase their general knowledge. All books are written, reviewed, and leveled for guided reading and early reading intervention programs for use in shared, guided, and independent reading and writing activities to support a balanced approach to literacy instruction.

TO ADULT HELPERS

The projects in this title are fun and simple. There are just a few things to remember to keep kids safe. Some projects require the use of sharp or hot objects. Also, kids may be using messy materials such as glue or paint. Make sure they protect their clothes and work surfaces. Review the projects before starting, and be ready to assist when necessary.

KEY SYMBOLS

Watch for these warning symbols in this book. Here is what they mean.

HOT!
You will be working with something hot. Get help!

SHARP!
You will be working with a sharp object. Get help!

CONTENTS

WHAT IS BIOFUEL?

Biofuel is an energy source produced from plant and animal matter. The matter used to make biofuel is called biomass.

SUGARCANE FIELD

Biomass has different sources. Crops are one source of biomass. Sugarcane, corn, and soybeans are common biomass crops.

Another source of biomass is dry plant matter. This can include trees, grasses, and farm waste.

CORN FIELD

Biofuel is a renewable **resource**. Plants and animals are always growing. So, biofuels can be produced quickly.

But growing and producing biofuels uses **fossil fuels**, such as **petroleum**. This harms the **environment**.

Biofuels are also costly to produce. Scientists are working to make biofuels cheaper and better for the environment.

FARM WASTE

TYPES OF BIOFUELS

Biomass is taken to biofuel **refineries**. There, it is processed into biofuel. Two common biofuels are ethanol and biodiesel. These are both used to power cars and other machines.

ETHANOL

Most ethanol is made from corn or sugarcane. Sugar is removed from the plants. Then the sugar is **fermented**. This is a chemical process that breaks down the sugar. This produces several **substances**, including ethanol.

ETHANOL REFINERY

SOYBEANS

BIODIESEL

Oil from animal fats or plants such as soybeans are used to make biodiesel. The oil is separated out. Then it is mixed with an alcohol in a chemical process. This produces biodiesel.

FUEL MIXES

Ethanol and biodiesel are often combined with other fuels. These include gasoline and diesel fuel made from **petroleum**. Then the fuel is sent to gas stations for people to buy and use.

E10 FUEL IS 10 PERCENT ETHANOL

BIOFUEL HISTORY

The most basic biofuel is wood. People have burned wood for heat, light, and cooking for thousands of years. Whale oil is another biofuel. People used it to light lamps in the 1700s and 1800s.

Cars were first invented in the 1800s. Their engines used different kinds of fuel. Some used oils from plants. The Ford Model T car could run on ethanol.

But soon, fuel made from **petroleum** became standard for car engines and many other machines. These fuels included gasoline and diesel fuel.

FORD MODEL T

RUDOLF DIESEL

Rudolf Diesel was a German engineer. He invented the diesel engine in 1893. His first models ran on vegetable or peanut oil. Later diesel engines used petroleum diesel fuel. Diesel engines are still used today in trains and large trucks. Some of these engines now run on biodiesel fuel.

Today, people worry about pollution caused by **petroleum** and other **fossil fuels**. People also worry that fossil fuels could get used up.

These concerns have led to greater interest in biofuels. Scientists are working to make biofuels better for the **environment**.

MODERN DIESEL ENGINE

MATERIALS

Here are some of the materials that you will need for the projects in this book.

ARTIFICIAL SWEETENER

BOTTLE OPENER

CAN OPENER

CARD STOCK

CORK

CORN SYRUP

DARNING NEEDLE

DOUBLE-SIDED TAPE

FELT

FUNNEL

HONEY

INSTANT YEAST

KNITTING NEEDLES

LIGHTER

MASON JAR

MEASURING CUPS & SPOONS

METAL CAN

MORTAR & PESTLE

PEANUTS

PLASTIC ZIPPER BAG

PLIERS

STOPWATCH

SUNFLOWER SEEDS

TEST TUBES & TEST TUBE RACK

THERMOMETER

BUTTER CANDLES

MATERIALS: stick of butter, dinner knife, string, ruler, scissors, darning needle, ceramic plate, lighter or matches

In the 1700s, many people used oils or fats for lighting. They would burn these oils to produce light. Butter is made of fat. It can be used for lighting too!

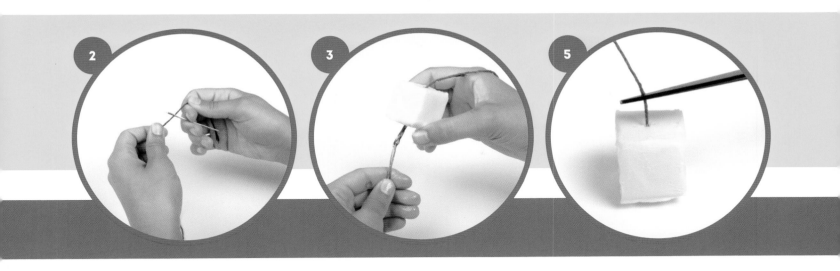

① Cut the stick of butter into four equal pieces.

② Cut a piece of string about 8 inches (20 cm) long. Thread the string on the needle.

③ Stick the needle through the center of a piece of butter. Pull it all the way through.

④ Keep pulling until the end of the string is inside the butter.

⑤ Trim the string ¼ inch (0.6 cm) from the top of the butter. This is the butter candle's wick.

⑥ Repeat steps 2 through 5 with the other butter pieces.

⑦ Set the butter candles on the plate. Have an adult light the wicks of your candles. Watch them glow!

PLANT DECOMPOSITION

MATERIALS: vegetable scraps (peels, cobs, cores & other food), plant scraps (twigs, lawn clippings, leaves), non-latex gloves (optional), large mason jar, notebook, pencil, camera (optional)

Plants must be broken down so that their sugars can be used to make biofuel. Making a **compost** jar shows how quickly plants **decompose**. Certain plant materials break down more quickly than others. These plants may work well as biofuels!

① Tear the vegetable and plant scraps into small pieces. You could wear gloves to keep your hands clean.

② Put a layer of vegetable scraps in the jar.

③ Add a layer of plant scraps.

④ Keep adding layers of vegetable and plant scraps until the jar is full.

⑤ Observe the scraps in the jar. What do they look like? Write down your observations. You could draw pictures or take photographs too!

⑥ Seal the jar tightly.

⑦ Set the jar in a warm place.

⑧ Check on the jar each day. Observe how it changes. Which materials **decompose** the fastest? Record the changes in your notebook.

OIL EXTRACTION

MATERIALS: sunflower seeds, spoon, mortar & pestle, measuring spoons, water, test tube, test tube rack, funnel, ruler

Certain biofuels use oil from plants. The oil needs to be **extracted** and separated. One kind of oil is sunflower oil. This comes from sunflower seeds. Sunflower oil is used in biodiesel.

① Put a spoonful of sunflower seeds in the mortar. Grind the seeds with the pestle.

② Stir in 4 teaspoons of water.

③ Put a test tube in a test tube rack. Set a funnel in the test tube. Spoon the wet, ground seeds into the test tube.

④ Add another teaspoon of water to the mortar. Swish the water around to rinse the mortar. Pour this water into the test tube.

⑤ Put the stopper in the test tube.

⑥ Let the test tube sit for two days. Observe it occasionally as the plant oil separates.

⑦ Once the liquid has totally separated, measure how much oil you produced!

BIOFUEL BAGS

MATERIALS: 5 small plastic zipper bags, permanent marker, water, 5 spoons, instant yeast, sugar, corn syrup, honey, artificial sweetener, stopwatch, paper, pencil

Ethanol is made from sugar. This sugar often comes from corn. But ethanol can be made from other sources too!

1. Label the five bags "control," "sugar," "corn syrup," "honey," and "artificial."

2. Fill each bag halfway with warm water.

3. Add a spoonful of yeast to each bag.

Continued on the next page.

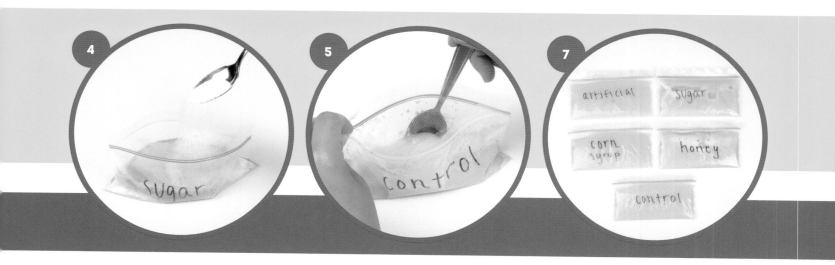

4 Add a spoonful of each sweetener to the bag with the matching label. Use a clean spoon for each sweetener. Don't add anything to the control bag.

5 Stir the contents of each bag until the **substances** are completely **dissolved**.

6 Seal the bags. Make sure there is no air in them.

7 Set the bags down with the labels facing up.

8 Observe the bags. After a few minutes, the contents will start to grow.

9 Start the stopwatch. Write down your observations. What do the bags look like? What do the substances inside the bags look like? Do you hear or smell anything?

10 Check the bags every 5 minutes. Write down your observations each time.

11 Write your final observations after 20 minutes. Which bag grew the most? Which grew the least?

Ethanol is made from sugar. The sugar usually comes from corn or sugarcane. The plant is ground into small grains. Water is added to create a mash. Then **enzymes** are added to the mash. This separates out the sugars. Then yeast is added. This causes **fermentation**. Fermentation creates ethanol and carbon dioxide. The mixture is distilled. This process separates out the ethanol and removes any water from it. Then it is ready to fuel **vehicles**.

1. MILLING
Biomass is ground up.

2. MASHING
Water and enzymes separate out the sugar.

3. FERMENTING
Yeast causes the sugar to ferment.

4. DISTILLING
Ethanol is separated out. All of the water is removed. The ethanol is prepared for use as fuel.

5. TRANSPORT
The ethanol is sent to gas stations and other users.

PEANUT ENERGY

MATERIALS: large empty metal can, can opener, bottle opener, pliers, small empty metal can, measuring cup, water, needle, cork, shelled peanuts, thermometer, paper, pencil, metal skewer or knitting needle, ceramic plate, lighter or matches

Biofuels are burned. This **releases** the chemical energy stored in the biomass. The energy can be used to produce heat.

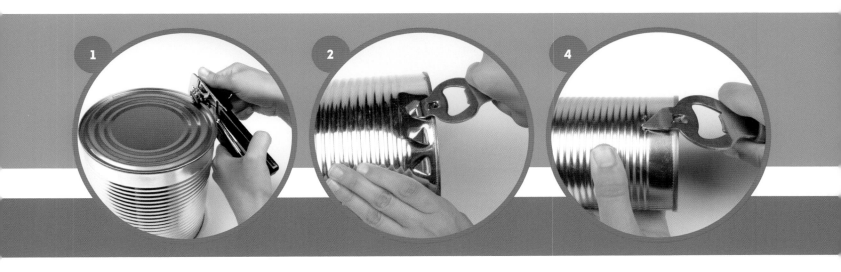

1 Remove the top and bottom of the large metal can.

2 Use the point of a bottle opener to make holes around one end of the large can.

3 Flatten the pointed edges of the can's holes with a pliers so they won't poke you.

4 Use the bottle opener to make two holes near the top of the small can. The holes should be directly opposite each other.

Continued on the next page.

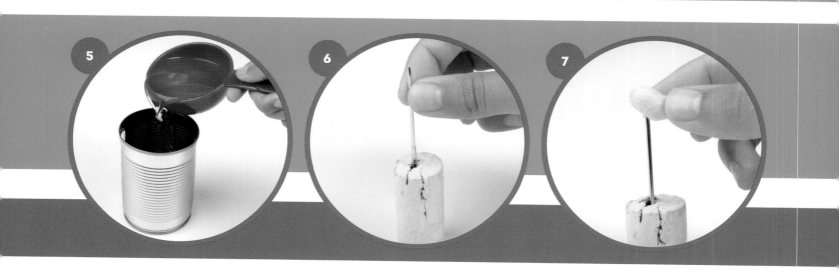

5   Pour ½ cup of water into the small can. Let the water sit for an hour so it reaches room temperature.

6   Push the eye end of the needle into the narrower end of the cork.

7   Stick a peanut onto the point of the needle. Try to put the peanut on at a slight angle. The peanut might break. That's okay! Just try it again with a new peanut.

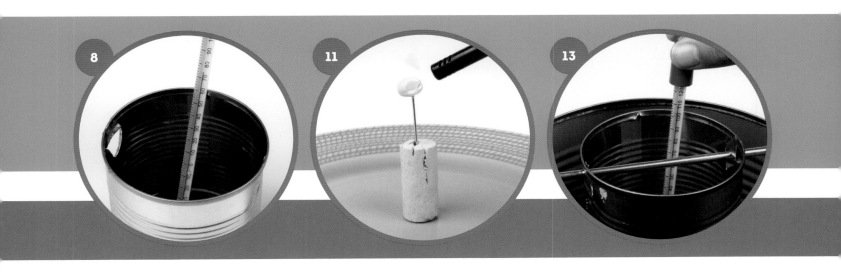

8 Use a thermometer to measure the water temperature. Write down the temperature.

9 Slide the metal skewer through the two holes in the small can. Set the skewer across the end of the large can without the holes. The small can should hang inside the large can.

10 Set the cork on the plate with the peanut pointing up. Place the large can over the cork. If the small can touches the peanut, cut the bottom of the cork to make it shorter.

11 Remove the can. Have an adult light the peanut.

12 Quickly place the can back over the cork. Let the peanut burn for a few minutes or until it goes out.

13 Measure the temperature of the water again. How much did it change?

FELT ALGA MODEL

MATERIALS: bowl that is about 5 inches (20 cm) across, green, yellow & red felt, marker, scissors, double-sided tape, blue card stock, white paper

A new biofuel source is **algae**. Algae are plant-like organisms. Like plants, algae use the sun's energy to take in carbon dioxide and **release** oxygen. This process is called photosynthesis. Photosynthesis can also produce ethanol.

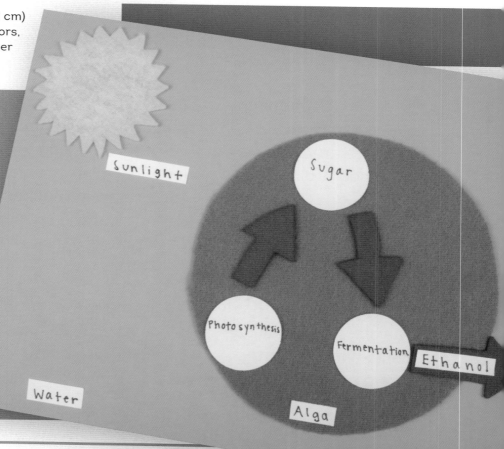

Sunlight

Sugar

Photosynthesis

Fermentation

Ethanol

Water

Alga

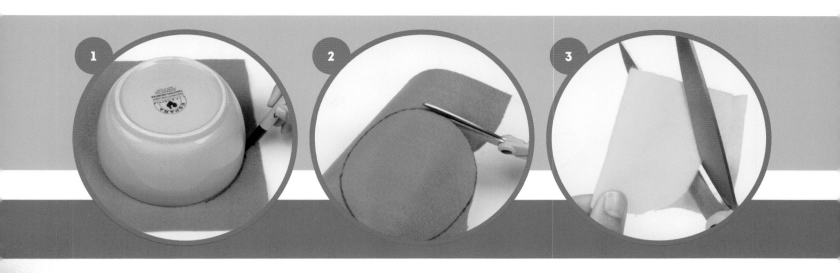

① Set the bowl upside down on a piece of green felt. Trace around it.

② Cut out the circle. This is your **alga** cell.

③ Cut a piece of yellow felt smaller than the green circle. Fold it in half. Cut a semicircle at the fold.

Continued on the next page.

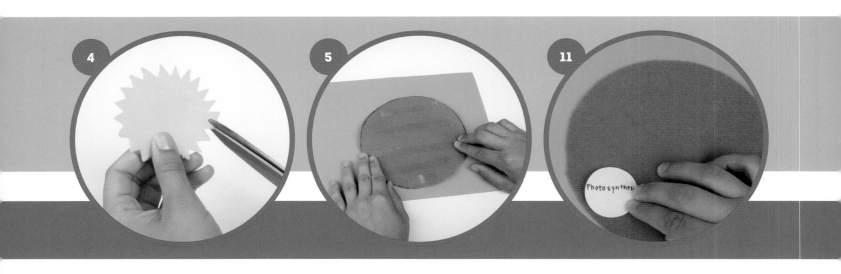

4 Unfold the felt. Cut zigzags along the edges. This is the sun!

5 Use double-sided tape to stick the cell near the bottom of the blue card stock.

6 Tape the sun near the top of the card stock.

7 Cut four small rectangles out of paper. Label them "Sunlight," "Water," "Ethanol," and "**Alga**."

8 Tape the "Sunlight" label near the sun. Tape the "Water" label to the blue card stock.

9 Draw three arrow shapes on red felt. Cut them out.

10 Cut three small circles out of paper. Label them "Photosynthesis," "Sugar," and "**Fermentation**."

11 Tape the "Photosynthesis" circle near the edge of the cell.

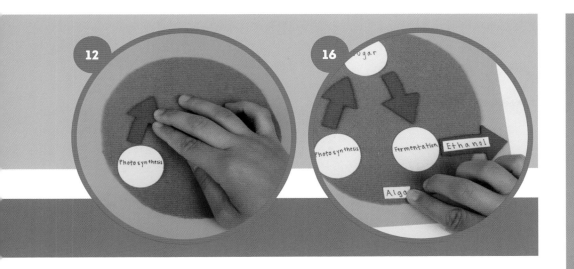

12 Tape an arrow pointing up from the circle.

13 Tape the "Sugar" circle at the end of the arrow. Tape the second arrow pointing down from the "Sugar" circle.

14 Tape the "**Fermentation**" circle at the end of the second arrow.

15 Tape the third arrow pointing away from the "Fermentation" circle and out of the cell.

16 Tape the "Ethanol" label on the last arrow. Tape the "**Alga**" label at the bottom of the cell.

17 Follow the felt model's path. This is how algae produce ethanol!

Photosynthesis creates sugar. The sugar is stored in the algae's cells. Sometimes, the sugar is fermented in the cells. This makes ethanol.

Algae can only make a small amount of ethanol naturally. Scientists help them produce more by fermenting the algae with yeast or other **substances**.

Algae also produce oils that can be used to make biodiesel.

Scientists believe algae could be a better source of fuel than other types of biomass. Algae could become an important biomass.

CONCLUSION

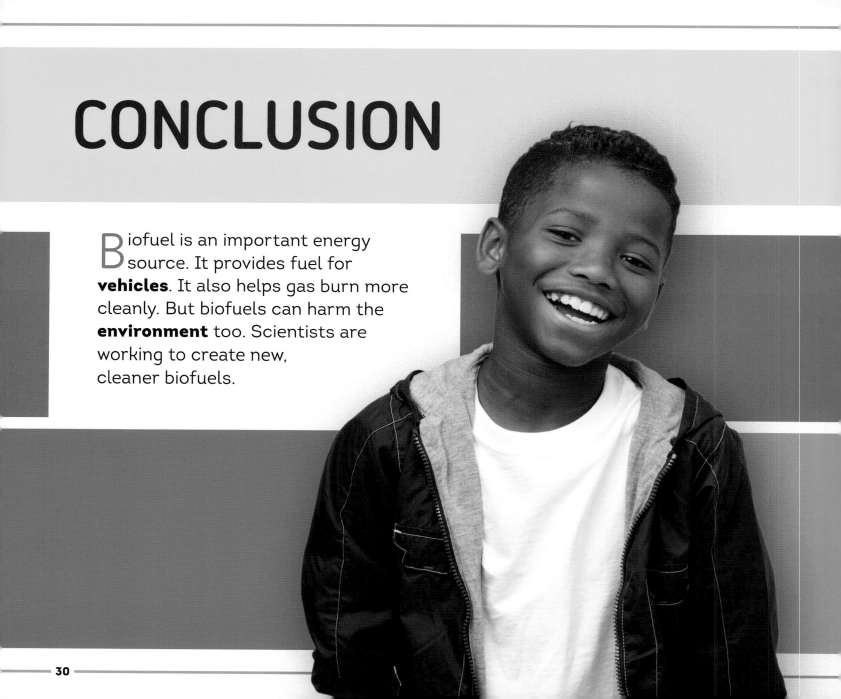

Biofuel is an important energy source. It provides fuel for **vehicles**. It also helps gas burn more cleanly. But biofuels can harm the **environment** too. Scientists are working to create new, cleaner biofuels.

QUIZ

1. Biofuels come from rocks. **TRUE OR FALSE?**

2. What are two common biofuels?

3. Who invented the diesel engine in 1893?

LEARN MORE ABOUT IT!

You can find out more about biofuel energy at the library. Or you can ask an adult to help you **research** biofuel energy on the internet!

Answers: 1. False   2. Ethanol and biodiesel   3. Rudolf Diesel

GLOSSARY

alga – a plant or plant-like organism that lives in water.

compost – a mixture of natural materials, such as food scraps and lawn clippings, that can turn into fertilizer over time.

decompose – to break down or rot.

dissolve – to become part of a liquid.

environment – nature and everything in it, such as the land, sea, and air.

enzyme – a chemical substance in animals and plants that helps cause natural processes.

extract – to get out by pressing, distilling, or by a chemical process.

ferment – to undergo a chemical process that turns sugar into other products. This process is called fermentation.

fossil fuel – a fuel formed in Earth from the remains of plants or animals. Coal, oil, and natural gas are fossil fuels.

petroleum – a dark-colored liquid that is a fossil fuel. It is used to make fuel, plastics, and other products.

refinery – a place where unwanted parts of something are removed to make it usable or valuable.

release – to set free or let out.

research – to find out more about something.

resource – something that is usable or valuable.

substance – anything that takes up space, such as a solid object or a liquid.

vehicle – something used to carry persons or large objects. Examples include cars, trucks, and buses.